W9-BRC-264

AMERICA
THE BEAUTIFUL

SCHOLASTIC INC.

Cartwheel BOOKS®

New York Toronto London Auckland Sydney Mexico City New Delhi Hong Kong Buenos Aires

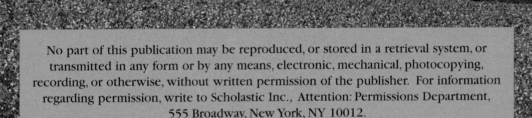

Photography credits for *America the Beautiful*:
Cover: top left: Joseph Sohm/Stone; top right: SuperStock; bottom right: SuperStock; bottom left: SuperStock
Back cover: Lori Adamski Peek/Stone
Pages: 2-3: Bob Rowan; Progressive Image/Corbis; 4-5: FPG; 6-7 background: Darrell Gulin; 6: W. Wayne Lockwood, M.D./Corbis; 7: Paul Stover/Sto
8-9: SuperStock; 10: SuperStock; 11 top left: SuperStock; 11, top right: SuperStock; 11, bottom right: SuperStock; 11, bottom left: Stephanie
Maze/Corbis; 12-13, background: Keven R. Morris/Corbis; 12, top row left: Michael Townsend/Stone; 12, top row middle: Cosmo Condina/Ston
12, top row right: FPG; 12, middle row left: Joseph Pobereskin/Stone; 12, middle row right: Mike Zens/Corbis; 12, bottom row left: FPG; 12, bott
row right: Steve Raymer/Corbis; 13, top left: SuperStock; 13, top right: SuperStock; 13, second row left, FPG; 13, second row center: David
Muench/Stone; 13, second row right: Dallas and John Heaton/Corbis; 13, third row left, Wolfgang Kaehler/Corbis; 13, third row right: FPG;
13, bottom left: Harvey Lloyd/FPG; 13, bottom right: Toyohiro Yamada/FPG; 14-15: Doug Wilson/Corbis; 16: SuperStock; 17: Joseph Sohm/Stone
18, top: Lori Adamski Peek/Stone; 18, bottom left: Lori Adamski Peek/Stone; 18, bottom right: Lori Adamski Peek/Stone; 19: Stephen Simpson/FP
20: Bruce Hands/Stone; 21: Jake Rajs/Stone; 22-23: Darrell Gulin/Stone; 24: David Young Wolff/PhotoEdit.

No part of this publication may be reproduced, or stored in a retrieval system, or transmitted in any form or by any means, electronic, mechanical, photocopying, recording, or otherwise, without written permission of the publisher. For information regarding permission, write to Scholastic Inc., Attention: Permissions Department, 555 Broadway, New York, NY 10012.

ISBN 0-439-39963-7

Copyright © 2001 by Scholastic Inc.
All rights reserved. Published by Scholastic Inc.
SCHOLASTIC, CARTWHEEL BOOKS, and associated logos are trademarks and/or registered trademarks of Scholastic Inc.

10 9 8 7 6 5 4 3   2 3 4 5 /6

Printed in the U.S.A.   08
First printing, September 2001

O beautiful

For spacious skies,

For amber waves of grain,

For purple mountain majestie

Above the fruited plain!

America! America!

God shed his grace on thee,

And crown thy good

With brotherhood

From sea to shining sea!

O beautiful
For spacious skies,
 For amber waves of grain,
  For purple mountain majesties
  Above the fruited plain!
   America! America!
    God shed his grace on thee,
    And crown thy good
    With brotherhood
     From sea to shining sea!